DK READERS

Level 2

A Note to Parents

DK READERS is a compelling program for beginning readers, designed in conjunction with leading literacy experts, including Dr. Linda Gambrell, Distinguished Professor of Education at Clemson University. Dr. Gambrell has served as President of the National Reading Conference, the College Reading Association, and the International Reading Association.

Beautiful illustrations and superb full-color photographs combine with engaging, easy-to-read stories to offer a fresh approach to each subject in the series. Each DK READER is guaranteed to capture a child's interest while developing his or her reading skills, general knowledge, and love of reading.

The five levels of DK READERS are aimed at different reading abilities, enabling you to choose the books that are exactly right for your child:

Pre-level 1: Learning to read
Level 1: Beginning to read
Level 2: Beginning to read alone
Level 3: Reading alone
Level 4: Proficient readers

The "normal" age at which a child begins to read can be anywhere from three to eight years old. Adult participation through the lower levels is very helpful for providing encouragement, discussing storylines, and sounding out unfamiliar words.

No matter which level you select, you can be sure that you are helping your child learn to read, then read to learn!

LONDON, NEW YORK, MUNICH,
MELBOURNE, and DELHI

Created by Leapfrog Press Ltd
Project Editor Naia Bray-Moffatt
Art Editor Jane Horne
For DK Publishing
Senior Editor Linda Esposito
Senior Art Editor Diane Thistlethwaite
U.S. Editor Regina Kahney
Pre-production Francesca Wardell
Picture Researcher Liz Moore
Photographer Andy Crawford

Ballet Consultant
Alison Good

Reading Consultant
Linda B. Gambrell, Ph.D.

First American Edition, 1999
This edition, 2013
Published in the United States by DK Publishing
375 Hudson Street, New York, New York 10014

13 14 15 16 17 10 9 8 7 6 5 4 3 2 1
002—192120—July/2013

A catalog record for this book is available
from the Library of Congress.
ISBN: 978-1-4654-0942-3 (Paperback)
ISBN: 978-1-4654-0943-0 (Hardcover)

DK books are available at special discounts when purchased in bulk
for sales promotions, premiums, fund-raising, or educational use.
For details, contact:
DK Publishing Special Markets
375 Hudson Street, New York, New York 10014
SpecialSales@dk.com

Color reproduction by Colourscan, Singapore
Printed and bound in China by L Rex Printing Co., Ltd.
The publisher would like to thank the following
for their kind permission to reproduce their photographs:
Key: t=top, a=above, b=below, l=left, r=right, c=center
Camera Press: 9br; /Andrew Crickmay: 31tr; Mary Evans Picture
Library: 5br; Royal Opera House/Catherine Ashmore: 25tr Models:
Amy Berry, Naia Bray-Moffatt, Rosie Fisher, Alison Good, Robyn
Hewitt, Alex Johns, Lizzie Knight, Siobhan McCleod, Guy and Jack
Westbrook, and Olivia and Grace Williams. In addition, Dorling
Kindersley would like to thank: Avril Mills for permission to
photograph in her ballet studio, Dance-A-Ramix. Gill Cossey and
Monica Clark of Chameleons Face Painting, Woking.

Discover more at
www.dk.com

DK READERS

BEGINNING TO READ ALONE 2

The Little
Ballerina

Written by Sally Grindley

DK

Laura pulled on her leotard
in front of her bedroom mirror.
She bent her legs
and then stood again.
It was a perfect plié (plee-AY).

"Hurry up!"
said Laura's mother.
"You don't want
to be late for
ballet school today."

French names
Ballet steps have French names
because they were first written
down in France more than 300
years ago. French king Louis XIV
(1638–1715) danced in several ballets.

Laura opened a closet and
took out her best ballet shoes.
Today the school
was putting on a show—
The Big Bad Dog and the
Two Little Kittens.

Ballet shoes

For practicing, ballet dancers wear leather or canvas shoes held on with ribbons or elastic. Satin shoes are usually worn only for shows.

Laura had a part as a rabbit. She couldn't wait to dance in her first show.

"Good luck," said Laura's mom on the way to school.

At the school, Laura looked for
her best friend, Miranda.
But she didn't see
Miranda anywhere.
The other children
chatted happily
as they put on
their shoes.

"In you come,"
said their teacher, Mrs. Beth.
"Straight to the barre and warm up."
Laura stood at the wooden rail.
"Where's Miranda?" she said
to herself.

Using the barre
Dancers hold on to
the barre, the wooden
rail, to keep steady
while they practice.

"Hold on to the barre," said Mrs. Beth. "Feet in first position. And gentle pliés in time to the music."

Laura knew all five positions by heart:

In first position, your heels touch and your toes turn out to the side.

First position

Second position

In second position, your feet are apart.

Third position

In third position, the heel of one foot goes halfway in front of the other foot.

In fourth position, the right foot goes in front of the left, a foot's length between them.

Fourth position

Fifth position

In fifth position, your front foot is placed flat against your back foot.

Laura tried hard
as she did her
steps at the barre.

Then the class
did arm movements.

"Let your head and eyes
follow the movements
of your arms,"
called out Mrs. Beth.
Laura moved
her hands
lightly around
her body.

"We'll stop there,"
called out Mrs. Beth.
"Come and sit down."

Laura sat on the floor
with the other dancers.
"Poor Miranda
has hurt her foot.
She won't be able
to dance today."

The children gasped.
Miranda was one of the kittens.

Who would play her part?

"I'd like you to take her place, Laura.
You practiced all the steps
with Miranda."
Laura felt excited and scared.
She had one of the main parts
in the ballet now!

Laura's hands shook
as she put on Miranda's cat suit.
"Meow," said Kate, the other kitten.
"Meow," Laura giggled,
and felt a little better.

Just then Jane, the Big Bad Dog,
danced in on tiptoe.

Angie, the Good Witch, joined her.

"Hooray!" everyone cheered.

Jane and Angie were the best dancers
in the school.

While the other children put on their costumes, Laura practiced with Kate, Jane, and Angie.

Dancing on pointe
Older dancers with strong legs and feet wear pointe shoes. With pointe shoes they can dance on the tips of their toes.

At the end of the ballet
Laura had to do an arabesque
(ar-uh-BESK).
"Try one now," said Mrs. Beth.
Laura stood on one leg
with the other leg
stretched out behind.
Suddenly her ankle wobbled.

"You can do it," said Mrs. Beth.
"Stare at something
straight in front of you."
Laura stared at the clock
and lifted her leg again.
This time she didn't wobble.

"Makeup time!" called Mrs. Beth. She painted Kate and Laura's faces to look like kittens.

Then she checked everyone's
costumes and makeup.
"We're ready!" said Mrs. Beth.
"Walk to the hall
and wait behind the stage.
Good luck, everyone."

Laura stood in the wings
at the side of the stage.
Then the ballet began.

The Big Bad Dog
leaped across the stage
in a grand jeté (gron she-TAY).

The stage

Names are given to different parts of a stage. The wings are at either side of the stage.

Behind her came the Good Witch and the rest of Laura's class.

Then it was Laura's turn
to go on stage.
Her heart beat faster.
"Pas de chat," (pah de SHAH)
Laura said to herself
as she and Kate jumped sideways
across the stage like cats.

In the front row
Laura's mother looked surprised.
Laura was supposed
to be a rabbit!

Laura danced the steps
she had practiced.
The music helped her and
she began to feel like a kitten.
She forgot all about the audience.

Then it was time
for the arabesque.
Laura stood on one leg
and raised the other.

She felt her ankle wobble.
Then she saw a clock
in the wings.
She stared hard at it—
and balanced perfectly!

As the ballet ended
the audience began to clap.
Laura and the other dancers
took their bows.
Laura smiled at her mother,
who was clapping wildly.

Bow

Dancers bow to their teacher at the end of a class, or to the audience at the end of a show.

Laura thought being a ballet dancer was the best thing in the world!

Some ballet steps

Plié (plee-AY)
Movement in which
the knees bend.

Battement-tendus
(bat-MON ton-DOO)
Exercise in which the foot
is slid along the floor until it points.

Grand jeté
(gron she-TAY)
A big jump from
one leg to the other,
with legs outstretched
in the air.

Pas de chat
(pah de SHAH)
"Step of the cat":
a leap sideways.

Pirouette (peer-uh-WET)
A dancer spins around
on one leg.

Arabesque (ar-uh-BESK)
A dancer stands on one leg
and lifts the other straight up behind.

Index